Our Family Tree

Acknowledgments

Executive Editor: Diane Sharpe
Supervising Editor: Stephanie Muller
Design Manager: Sharon Golden
Page Design: Rafi Mohamed
Photography: Beamish, the North of England Open Air Museum:
pages 7, 9, 21; The Creative Publishing Company: cover (middle); Robert
Harding Picture Library: cover (bottom), page 27; The Hulton Deutsch
Collection: cover (top), pages 10, 17, 19, 23, 24.

ISBN 0-8114-3803-1

Our
Family
Tree

Mike Jackson

Illustrated by
Diana Bowles

STECK-VAUGHN ®
C O M P A N Y
ELEMENTARY • SECONDARY • ADULT • LIBRARY

4

Be careful with those photo albums. Some
of the photos inside are very old.

That's your great-great-great-grandpa
Samuel. That picture was taken about
one hundred years ago.

Here he is fixing a shoe on a horse's hoof.
He was a blacksmith, just like his father.
Samuel was married to Agatha, so she was
your great-great-great-grandma. They
lived in England.

7

They are your great-great-grandma Maude and her two sisters, Ethel and Martha. Samuel and Agatha had seven children altogether. This photo just shows their daughters.

Maude was the first one of our relatives to move from England to the United States. She and your great-great-grandpa Stanley took a ship across the ocean. They became farmers in Kansas.

Ethel died when she was only 18. Back in those days, people often died young because they couldn't get medicine.

Let's take the albums downstairs, and I'll
draw you a family tree.

It's a map that shows how every relative fits into a family. It has dates to show when people were born and when they died.

Here is the first part of our family tree.

Great-Great-Great-
Grandpa Samuel
(1865-1950)

Great-Great-Great-
Grandma Agatha
(1870-1958)

Great-Great-
Grandma
Maude
(1893-1968)

Great-Great-
Grandpa
Stanley
(1887-1948)

Theodore
(1890-1957)

Wilfred
(1891-1917)

Ethel
(1892-1910)

Martha
(1894-1962)

Edward
(1896-1970)

George
(1902-1968)

Besides her two sisters, your great-great-grandma Maude also had four brothers. Their names were Theodore, Wilfred, Edward, and George.

That's a big family!

People often had big families back in those days.

Maude and Stanley had three children. Their names were Arthur, Winifred, and Edith. Winifred was your great-grandma.

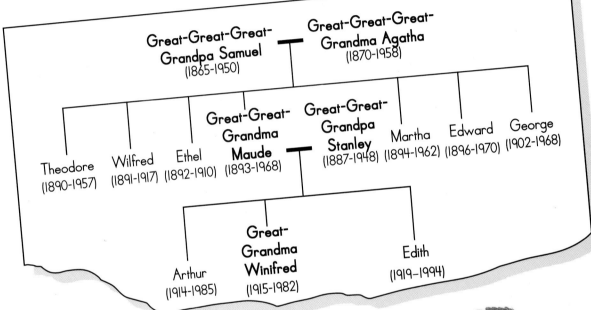

Great-Great-Great-Grandpa Samuel (1865-1950) — Great-Great-Great-Grandma Agatha (1870-1958)

Theodore (1890-1957)

Wilfred (1891-1917)

Ethel (1892-1910)

Great-Great-Grandma Maude (1893-1968) — Great-Great-Grandpa Stanley (1887-1948)

Martha (1894-1962)

Edward (1896-1970)

George (1902-1968)

Arthur (1914-1985)

Great-Grandma Winifred (1915-1982)

Edith (1919-1994)

Let's see if I can find a photo of your great-grandma.

Is this her, Grandma?

Look at the funny old car.

Yes, that is your great-grandma Winifred. She was my mother.

17

Here is your great-grandpa, my father.
His name was Frank.

What was his job?

18

He worked on a train. Here's a picture
of him and a friend in their train.

19

Who do you think this baby is?

It must be you, Grandma Betty!

What a funny old carriage!

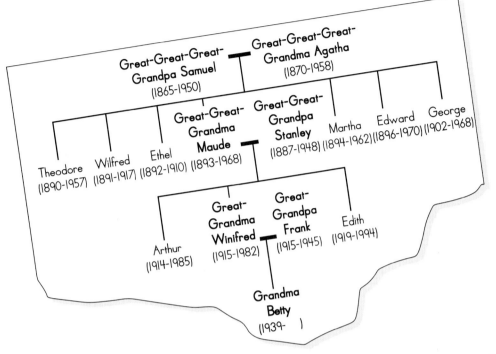

Great-Great-Great-Grandpa Samuel (1865-1950) — Great-Great-Great-Grandma Agatha (1870-1958)

Theodore (1890-1957)
Wilfred (1891-1917)
Ethel (1892-1910)

Great-Great-Grandma Maude (1893-1968) — Great-Great-Grandpa Stanley (1887-1948)

Martha (1894-1962)
Edward (1896-1970)
George (1902-1968)

Arthur (1914-1985)

Great-Grandma Winifred (1915-1982) — Great-Grandpa Frank (1915-1945)

Edith (1919-1994)

Grandma Betty (1939-   )

22

No, that's my brother Tom. My father is saying goodbye to him.

My father became a soldier and had to go away for a while.

Here's a picture of your grandpa Sidney and me on our wedding day. That was over thirty years ago.

You look very beautiful, Grandma.

What was Grandpa's job?

He was a shipbuilder. There aren't many shipbuilders anymore.

I'll bet you can't guess who the girl is in this photo!

I think it's Mom.

26

That must be
Uncle Paul with her.

We often went down to the seashore
when your mother was a child.

Now our family tree is almost finished. Who's missing?

That's right. Your names are missing. We'll put Tom, Kelly, and Tammy at the bottom.

Couldn't we draw another family tree, Grandma?

Yes, you could draw a family tree of your father's side of the family. Grandpa Peter may have some old pictures for you to see, too.

Here is Tom, Kelly, and Tammy's family tree. Five of the names are missing. Can you remember who the people are? The answers are on the last page, but don't look until you have tried naming everyone.

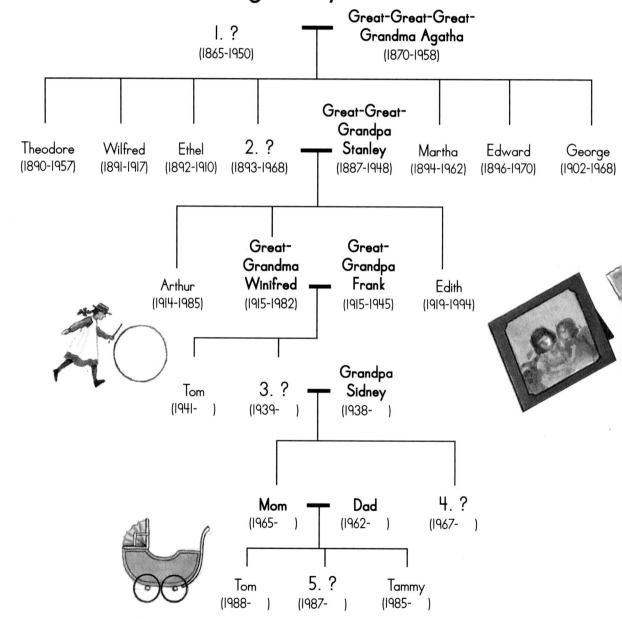

1. ?
(1865-1950)

Great-Great-Great-Grandma Agatha
(1870-1958)

Theodore
(1890-1957)

Wilfred
(1891-1917)

Ethel
(1892-1910)

2. ?
(1893-1968)

Great-Great-Grandpa Stanley
(1887-1948)

Martha
(1894-1962)

Edward
(1896-1970)

George
(1902-1968)

Arthur
(1914-1985)

Great-Grandma Winifred
(1915-1982)

Great-Grandpa Frank
(1915-1945)

Edith
(1919-1994)

Tom
(1941-)

3. ?
(1939-)

Grandpa Sidney
(1938-)

Mom
(1965-)

Dad
(1962-)

4. ?
(1967-)

Tom
(1988-)

5. ?
(1987-)

Tammy
(1985-)

30

Index

Answers: 1. Great-Great-Great-Grandpa Samuel 2. Great-Great-Grandma Maude 3. Grandma Betty 4. Uncle Paul 5. Kelly